MILITARY MISSIONS

PATROLLING

BY NEL YOMTOV

BELLWETHER MEDIA • MINNEAPOLIS, MN

EPIC

EPIC BOOKS are no ordinary books. They burst with intense action, high-speed heroics, and shadows of the unknown. Are you ready for an Epic adventure?

This edition first published in 2017 by Bellwether Media, Inc.

No part of this publication may be reproduced in whole or in part without written permission of the publisher.
For information regarding permission, write to Bellwether Media, Inc., Attention: Permissions Department, 5357 Penn Avenue South, Minneapolis, MN 55419.

Names: Yomtov, Nelson, author.
Title: Patrolling / by Nel Yomtov.
Description: Minneapolis, MN : Bellwether Media, Inc., 2017. | Series: Epic:
   Military Missions | Includes bibliographical references and index. |
Audience:
   Grades 2-7.
Identifiers: LCCN 2016000250 | ISBN 9781626174351 (hardcover
: alk. paper)
Subjects: LCSH: Combat–Juvenile literature. | United States–Armed
   Forces–Infantry–Drill and tactics–Juvenile literature. | Military
   reconnaissance–Juvenile literature.
Classification: LCC U165 .Y66 2017 | DDC 355.4/13–dc23
LC record available at http://lccn.loc.gov/2016000250

Printed in the United States of America, North Mankato, MN.

TABLE OF CONTENTS

RAID!

A patrol of United States Army soldiers watches a small house in Iraq. The patrol has been sent to search the house. There may be weapons and **explosives** hidden there.

TURKEY

SYRIA

IRAN

IRAQ

JORDAN

SAUDI ARABIA

KUWAIT

N
W E
S

Enemy soldiers fire at the patrol from inside the house. The Americans fire back. They drive the enemy away.

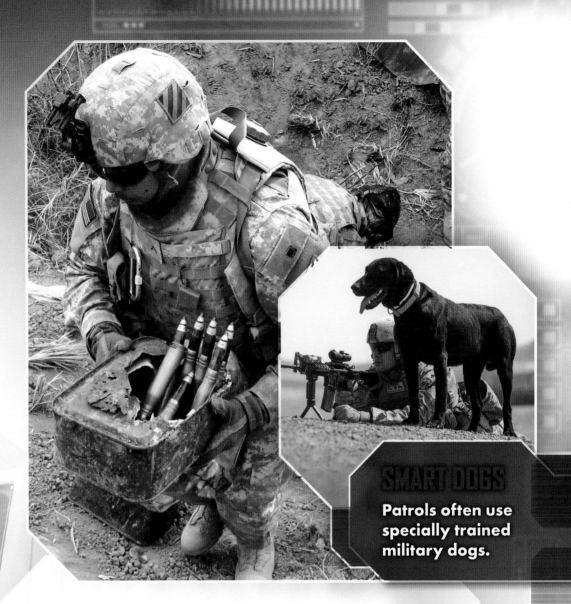

Patrols often use specially trained military dogs.

The patrol takes what is found in the house. Then the team returns safely to the main fighting force.

THE MISSION

Patrols are small groups of soldiers. These small groups complete tasks that are part of a bigger mission.

When a patrol finishes a task, the soldiers return to the main fighting force. They report to their leader.

There are different kinds of patrols.
Combat patrols fight enemies.
They may take enemy supplies.
Recon patrols gather information.
They find out about an area or an
enemy's location.

recon patrol

FOCUS RALLY

Sometimes a patrol needs to
regroup. The team meets at a
rally point, or meeting place.

REAL-LIFE PATROLLING

What: Operation Neptune Spear

Who: U.S. Navy SEAL Team Six

Where: Abbottabad, Pakistan

When: May 1, 2011

Why: Remove the leader of al-Qaeda, a terrorist group

How: U.S. Navy SEALs and Army helicopters used gathered intelligence to perform a successful raid on the hideout of Osama bin Laden, leader of al-Qaeda

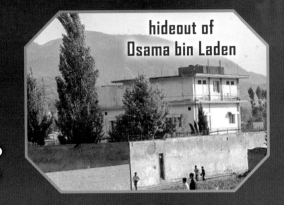

hideout of Osama bin Laden

combat patrol

THE PLAN

Every patrol is prepared to fight. Soldiers carry weapons like **carbines** or **grenades**.

grenade

During **raids**, some use a **door charge**. It can blow open locked doors.

Recon patrols move quietly. Soldiers use **hand signals** to talk with one another. They try to avoid contact with the enemy. They use maps and **binoculars** to gather **intelligence**.

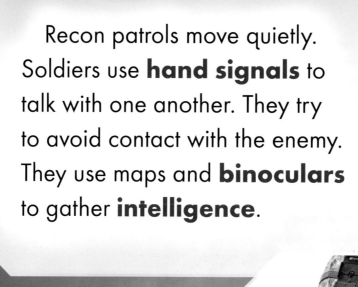

Claymore mine

M4 carbine

grenade

M320 grenade launcher

infantry mobility vehicle

THE TEAM

All branches of the U.S. military use patrols. Patrols serve in cities and **rural** areas. They work on mountains and waterways. They also work in deserts, jungles, and forests.

HELP FROM DOLPHINS

The U.S. Navy sometimes uses dolphins to do underwater recon. Cameras are placed in the dolphins' mouths.

All U.S. military troops learn patrol skills. They learn how to read maps and how to report information correctly. They also learn how to hide safely from the enemy.

SOLDIER PROFILE

A patrol member requires:
- **Courage**
- **Intelligence**
- **Calmness under pressure**
- **Reliability**
- **Discipline**
- **Fearlessness**

ACCOMPLISHED!

Patrolling is difficult. It requires careful planning. Patrols can help save the lives of the main fighting force. Their work is important to larger missions!

ON THE MOVE

Infantry mobility vehicles (IMVs) are often used for recon.

GLOSSARY

binoculars—handheld tools that let soldiers see things that are far away

carbines—small, lightweight guns

combat—fighting between soldiers or armies

door charge—a small bomb used to blow open a locked door

explosives—materials that blow up

grenades—small explosives that can be thrown by hand

hand signals—hand movements that mean something to another person

intelligence—information about an enemy's position, movements, or weapons

raids—surprise attacks

recon—a mission in which troops are sent to gather information about an enemy; recon is short for reconnaissance.

rural—related to the countryside

TO LEARN MORE

AT THE LIBRARY

Gordon, Nick. *Navy SEALs*. Minneapolis, Minn.: Bellwether Media, 2012.

Loria, Laura. *Marine Force Recon*. New York, N.Y.: Gareth Stevens Pub., 2012.

Slater, Lee. *Marine Force Recon*. Minneapolis, Minn.: ABDO Publishing, 2016.

ON THE WEB

Learning more about patrolling is as easy as 1, 2, 3.

1. Go to www.factsurfer.com.

2. Enter "patrolling" into the search box.

3. Click the "Surf" button and you will see a list of related web sites.

With factsurfer.com, finding more information is just a click away.

INDEX